The Hampstead Cookbook

Mariek,
with love
Freddie
x xx

Acknowledgments

The BookMaker would like to thank all of the people who kindly gave recipes to J. A. Steele of Hampstead for this book. We would also like to thank Frances Bissell, an award-winning cook and author of many books including *Entertaining*, *Modern Classics, and Organic Meat Cookbook* for her supportive words. Her column on food in the *Ham & High* appears monthly.

Published in 2003 by The BookMaker,
1 Colosseum Terrace, London NW1 4EB.

Design: Rachel Gibson
Cookery editor: Anne Sheasby
Location photography: Amanda Hancocks

Text © J. A. Steele of Hampstead

ISBN 0 9546379 0 9

Every effort has been made to ensure these recipes are accurate. However, due to differing conditions, and individual skills, the Publisher cannot be held responsible for any failures with the recipes.

Printed in Singapore

The Hampstead Cookbook

Edited by Lynn Bryan

Photography by Amanda Hancocks

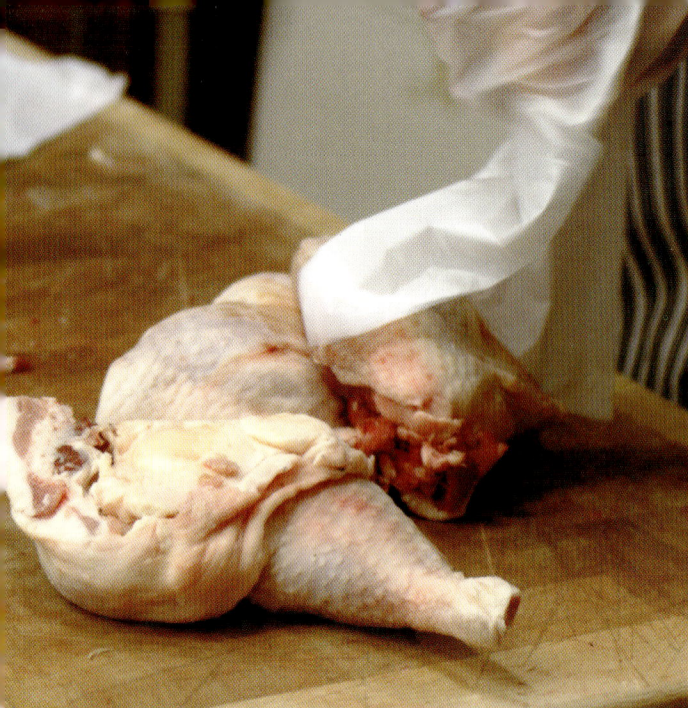

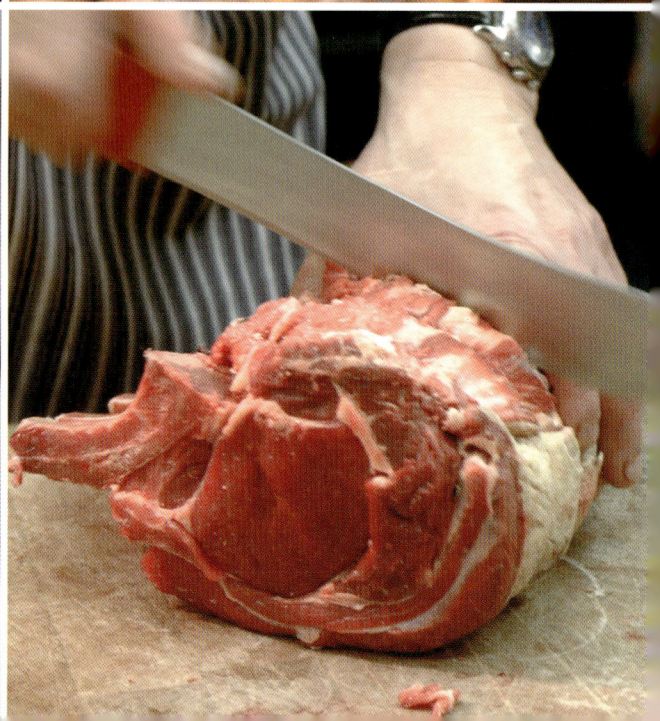

Contents

Foreword

Frances Bissell

I am delighted to write a few words to speed The Hampstead Cookbook on its way, into all our kitchens, and into those of our friends and families from all over the world, who have lived in, or visited, this special corner of London.

As a cook and cookery writer, it is important for me to be able to source good fresh ingredients, and Hampstead is special to me because I am able to shop every day if I need to, and buy my ingredients from professionals like Mr Steele and his team. It is such a treat to be able to buy meat from someone who knows his subject, who can tell you the age of the animal, where the lamb is from, how long the beef has been hung. And you can be sure that it will have been hung. If there were a register of authentic Hampstead treasures, Joe Steele would be at the top of the list.

The book goes some way to solving a riddle about our community which has puzzled me for many years, even before my husband, Tom, and I moved here more than twenty years ago. Why does Hampstead not have more good restaurants? Simple. It doesn't need them. Hampstead is full of good cooks, if Joe Steele's collection of recipes is anything to go by. I was impressed. These are seriously good recipes, and valuable because you know they have been tried and tested. Some of the recipes, contributed by our friends and neighbours, are accompanied by charming stories, which add to the pleasure of this excellent recipe collection, book-ended by practical advice on choosing and cooking meat from the Master Butcher himself.

Gillian Lawson's drawing of a snow-clad Flask Walk.

Introduction

Welcome to *The Hampstead Cookbook*. The idea was suggested as a way of celebrating J. A. Steele trading for more than thirty years in Flask Walk. What better way to mark the occasion than to produce a cookbook with recipes from my customers, plus a few of our own!

Memories flooded back when I was asked about the beginning of life in Hampstead Village. I came to look at the shop in 1969 and liked the area immediately, sensing it was the right place for a quality butcher's shop.

Flask Walk was a road then, with more shops along it. I have an old photograph of the Walk showing an overhead structure at the High Street end, with Hovis written across it. As you came in from the High Street, a pharmacy was located on the left-hand side, and a greengrocer. Culpepper's was past Kiki the hairdresser, and also a game restaurant, The Huntsman. Plus The Flask, which was always busy on Sundays. There were other butcher's shops in Hampstead, : Head's (opposite The Flask), Druce & Craddock were in the High Street, and Lidstone's. Sainsbury's was here, too.

Hampstead has always been an interesting area with writers, actors and actresses mingling with professors, lawyers and business people. Many of these wonderful characters have become my customers over the years. The actor Peter Barkworth was one of my first customers. John Hurt, who used to have the first house on the corner, was also one of our regulars, and Robert Powell.

Three jolly butchers: Eddie Keegan, Barry Steele and Mr Steele.

Barry Steele and pheasants.

Now the staff smirk quietly among themselves when I fail to recognise someone very famous and put my foot in it — I have even offered cooking times to the young wife of a famous chef! (She smiled, too.) So, you can guess we've had some amusing moments in the shop; in fact, we aim to be as amusing as possible to make the day pass quickly!

The Christmas queue has become famous for its sociability, despite the cold and occasional snowfall. A glass of good cheer and a mince pie helps keep the chill away! A few weddings have resulted from a chance meeting in the queue, and more than a few life-time friendships have sprung up while shoppers waited in line for their turkeys.

My customers make the business what it is. We have always aimed to serve, and to deliver what a customer wants and over the decades, their tastes have changed.

Both organic and free-range produce is in demand now. My customers are also more sophisticated than they were thirty years ago. When I started out, it was basic cuts for basic recipes. Now, they've been influenced by travel to France and Italy, to cities such as Marrakech, and all these cookery programmes, and books, which have created an interest in the exotic cuts.

Changes in lifestyle have meant a change in the style of eating. Recently we sold over about

170 kilos (300 lbs) of boneless chicken in a week. It's less fat, and light — the way we eat now since we became aware of health issues. However, you can't beat a beef casserole, a coq au vin, or a lamb stew on a cold winter's day.

The backyard barbecue, even with our (usually) unpredictable summer weather, has taken off. Americans and Australians brought the barbecue to Hampstead, fired it up, opened a can, grabbed the barbecue tongs and introduced great new ways with a piece of meat. It's heartening to know customers have fun with what you sell.

That sense of fun materialises on a Saturday when the shop doubles as a meeting place for young and old; the repartee flies fast and furious as parents, children and babies in pushchairs vie for space; and the dogs tethered to the metal hook outside look longingly at the plastic bags their masters carry out.

This book represents our customers' affection for the place meat has in their diet. There are short stories and recipes, plus information about meat cuts. The recipes have been tested them time and time again by their contributors. Thanks are due to each of them for their valued contribution to this book.

We hope you enjoy them and look forward to serving you again soon.

J. A. STEELE

Sirloin Steak
A fast-cooker, good grilled, barbecued or fried.

T-Bone Steak
A juicy slice that's good grilled, barbecued or fried.

A corner cut of topside roast
Slow-roast a piece of silverside and you can also salt it and boil it.

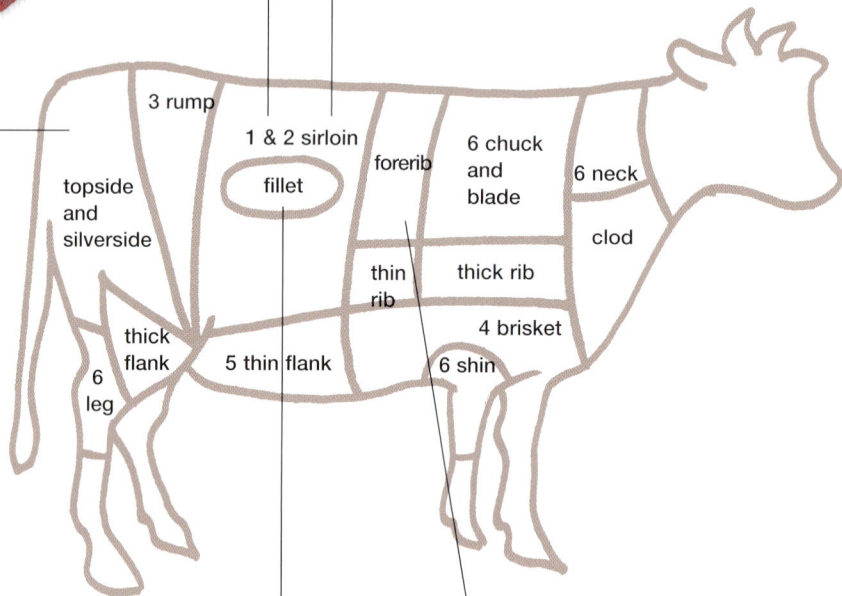

3 rump

1 & 2 sirloin

fillet

forerib

6 chuck and blade

6 neck

clod

topside and silverside

thin rib

thick rib

4 brisket

thick flank

6 leg

5 thin flank

6 shin

Fillet
Slices are good grilled, barbecued or fried. You can roast a whole fillet for a dinner party. Mince for Steak Tartare.

Forerib
The best bit for roasting.

Meat cuts: beef

Choosing the right cut for the dish you wish to make is the first step to successful cooking. To make it simple, the parts of an animal at the top of the body are the most tender, and the shoulder and lower legs, which get to move about a fair bit, are slightly tougher and usually cheaper. They need to be cooked for longer, too. Following is a guide to beef, lamb and pork cuts.

1. Sirloin (rolled) Good for roasting.

2. Porterhouse steak A big steak that's good grilled, barbecued or fried.

3. Rump Steak Good grilled, barbecued or fried. Best for stir-frying when cut into narrow strips.

4. Brisket (rolled) Good for pot-roasting.

5. Flank/Skirt Good for pot-roasting.

6. Leg, Shin, Chuck, Blade, Skirt, Neck Good for making casseroles and stews.

Preparing beef for a stew or casserole

Use a sharp knife to dice the meat. Trim off any unwanted fat, leaving a little for added flavour. Meat can shrink during cooking so it is best to dice the chunks larger than smaller. Cook slowly for a few hours for tenderness.

Mr Steele's Method of Cooking Steak

Wash the steak.and pat dry. Trim off any excess fat. Sprinkle a small amount of sea-salt and grind black pepper over both sides of the meat. (Add some freshly crushed garlic with a flat knife to one side if you like a garlic flavour.) Turn the hob on high. Place a heavy-bottomed frying pan on the hob and wait until it is hot. Add a spot of butter just to stop it sticking to the surface. Throw the steak into the frying pan and listen to it sizzle. Seal both sides. Cook for about three minutes each side if you like it rare to medium, and five minutes each side if you like it well done. If you have a smoke alarm in the kitchen, open all the doors!

Noisette

From the rack of lamb or loin, a noisette is a tender piece of lamb, is for roasting.

Rack of lamb

Good to roast and is just enough for two people. Two racks of lamb can be joined to make a crown roast or a guard of honour.

Leg of lamb

Good for roasting. Try butterflied lamb for a barbecue.

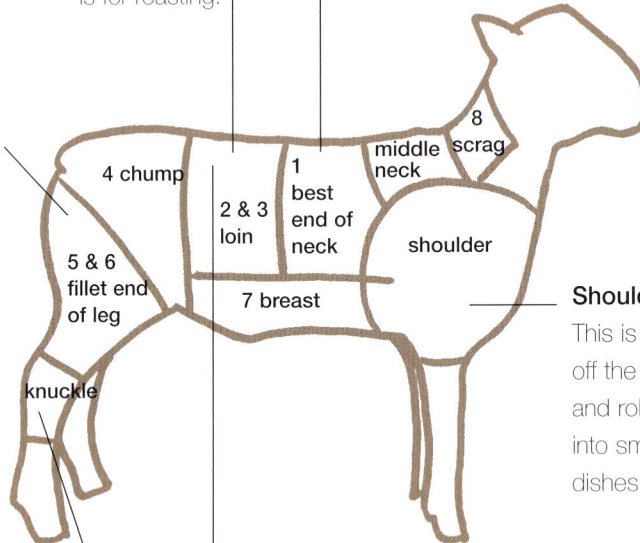

8 scrag

middle neck

1 best end of neck

4 chump

2 & 3 loin

shoulder

5 & 6 fillet end of leg

7 breast

knuckle

Shoulder

This is good for roasting (on and off the bone) and can be stuffed and rolled. It can also be cut into small pieces for braising dishes in a Morrocan-style.

Shank

From the knuckle, lamb shanks are good for braising and pot-roasting gently.

Saddle

Made up of two loins of lamb, it is good for roasting.

Meat cuts: lamb

1. Cutlet From the best end of neck area, small cutlets are great for grilling or frying.

2. Loin Great for roasting.

3. Loin chop Great for frying and grilling.

4. Chump chops Great for frying and grilling.

5. Leg fillet From the fillet end of leg, good for kebabs.

6. Leg steak A universal cut from the fillet end of the leg, it can be used for roasting, grilling, frying and braising. You can also cube it for a curry.

7. Boned breast (rolled) Good for roasting, and you can stuff it for extra flavour.

8. Scrag A bony piece, like middle neck, it is full of flavour and good for traditional stews and casseroles.

Choosing good lamb

When you're peering in the butcher's window, look for pieces of lamb cuts that are are not dry in appearance, nor too moist. Look for flesh that's not bloody, but more pinky brown. The fat ought to be white and look waxy. In England, the Spring lamb season starts around April and lasts through to midsummer. Look for a hint of blue in the H bone when buying.

Preparing lamb

The fat on a piece of lamb for roasting or grilling is an important part of the flavour. On a rack of lamb that will be cooked at high heat, the fat keeps the piece moist. If you are worried about fat, note some will drip off during the cooking, and you can always trim it after it is cooked.

Tenderloin or fillet
From the loin area, this is a lean cut and is good to grill, fry or barbecue.

Loin chop
Good for grilling, frying and to barbecue. If grilling, trim off as much fat as you want, and make a small cut in the fat to prevent the chop twisting as it cooks.

Loin
On the bone, or rolled, this is good for roasting, frying or grilling. Good for crackling, too.

Barbecue spare ribs
Known as American or Chinese-style spare ribs and come from the belly.

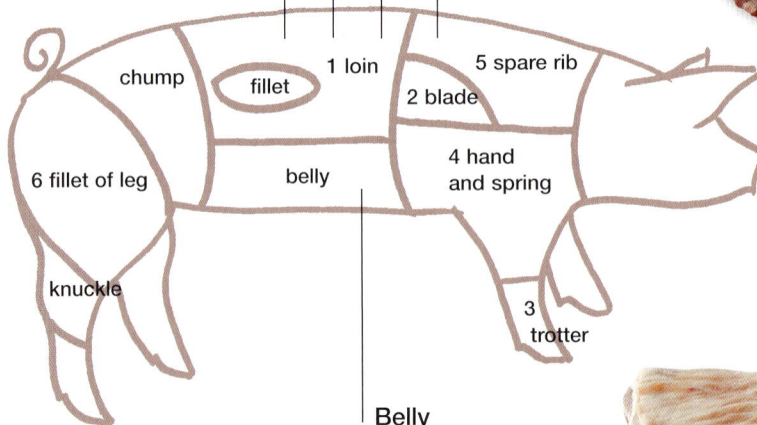

chump

fillet

1 loin

5 spare rib

2 blade

4 hand and spring

6 fillet of leg

belly

knuckle

3 trotter

Belly
Good to roast, braise, grill, fry and barbecue.

Meat cuts: pork

A superb piece of pork is a taste experience to be savoured. When cooked correctly, pork is juicy and tender. It helps to start with the right cut.

1. Medallion Cut from the tenderloin, it can be cooked quickly in the frying pan. Can also be grilled or barbecued.

2. Blade Good for roasting or braising and casseroles.

3. Trotter Considered a delicacy by some, this is boiled.

4. Hand and spring Can be roasted or braised.

5. Spare rib The spare rib chop is good for braising, grilling and frying.

6. Leg and leg fillet Good for roasting and makes a great Sunday joint for six or more.

Choosing good pork

The flesh should be dry with no hint of a slimy surface. Its colour should be a succulent pink, not too pale and not too dark. The fat should be white and firm. Its texture is important to achieve good crackling.

Hints on cooking pork

During the cooking process, the fat keeps the pork moist so trim your cut with this aspect in mind. Pork is a meat that benefits from slow cooking. Late cooking the main course? Then choose something else. Also, pork must be served well done. Use a skewer to text if a piece is cooked through. If the juice runs clear, then it is well cooked.

Chicken and poultry

This category encompasses chicken, poussins, guinea fowl, duck, goose, and turkey. Chicken is the nation's favourite meat by far because it is versatile. You can cook it any way you want! Free-range and organic chickens, sourced from France and England, have a distinct flavour and a firm texture. Corn-fed chickens are another taste sensation to be experienced. Hens are best for boiling.

Poussins Usually from 4 to 6 weeks old, these are small and cute, just perfect for two. Sourced in both France and England, they're tender and have a delicate flavour. When cooked their meat is soft, moist and pale. Excellent for roasting, they can also be grilled or fried.

Guinea fowl These are smaller and have less flesh than a chicken. Be careful not to dry a guinea fowl out when cooking it — it's best to lay strips of streaky bacon over the breast while roasting. Baste often. Good for pot-roasting and casseroles, too.

Duck Gressingham duck and French Barbary duck breasts are favourite choices. Usually the breasts have a layer of fat under which hides a dark and rich flesh. When cooking a breast, the fat drips out and creates a crisp skin. Best to roast duck.

Goose A traditional specialty popular at Christmas. Goose shrinks as it is cooked, with the fat melting away; however, a well-cooked goose is a flavour worth savouring.

Turkey The turkey has slightly darker flesh than a chicken. When cooked properly, it is moist and tender. Also available are rolled turkey breasts to roast and turkey breast steaks to grill or fry.

Choosing a good bird

Look for a bird with flesh that's firm in texture and looks dry, not shiny (frozen chickens and poultry that have been defrosted often look shiny).

Storing chicken and poultry

When you arrive home, take the poultry out of its packaging, wash it and pat dry. Take out any giblets that may be inside. Place the poultry on a clean plate. Lightly cover it with foil so nothing can drip on it from the shelves above. Place it in the refrigerator on a low shelf, away from other items. After handling and preparing raw chicken always wash your hands, as well as the chopping board, any preparation bowls and the knife you used.

Feathered and furred game

This category includes pheasant, partridge, quail, rabbit, hare, grouse, woodpigeon, mallard and venison. Autumn is the start of the season for these. The flavours are wide ranging, from the mild-tasting pheasant, partridge and quail to the wild-bird flavour of grouse and gamey venison. For wild game, it is essential to hang it for a period to help develop flavour. Ask your butcher to hang and prepare your wild game for you. Your choice might have a few imperfections on the outer flesh but these are to be expected if it is real game from the wild. Once prepared, you can roast game birds in the same way as you cook chicken.

Pheasant The season is from October 1 to February 1. Can be roasted or casseroled.

Partridge The season is from September 1 to February 1. These are small birds and feed two people sparingly. Can be roasted or casseroled.

Quail Available throughout the year, boneless or with bones. Lean creatures, they are excellent whether grilled, roasted or casseroled.

Grouse The season is from August 12 to December 10. These small birds feed one per person. Can be roasted or casseroled.

Woodpigeon These are available throughout the year, and have dark, full-flavoured flesh. If you are roasting or grilling them, perhaps marinade them for tenderness and a moist flesh. Good to casserole with herbs and wine.

Mallard The season is from September 1 to January 31. A common wild duck, it has less fat than a farmyard duck and more flavour. Roast or casserole.

Venison All venison is lean. The main cuts are shoulder, which can be rolled, loin chop, loin,haunch and leg steak (from the lower haunch). If roasting, keep it moist by basting. The haunch is good for roasting, as are the loin and saddle. For frying, try saddle steaks and leg steaks and chops. Steak and chops are good for grilling; however, do not over cook or it will become dry.

Rabbit Sourced from France or England, the versatile rabbit can be roasted, or grilled, and is great in casseroles and stews. Sold whole.

Hare This has a gamey flavour, much more than rabbit. Can be roasted or casseroled. Sold whole.

beef
recipes

Ms. Hamburger's barbecued hamburger

A variety of the infamous 'Sloppy Joe', adored by males (my twin sons eat five sandwiches each at one sitting; I always double this recipe) and suitable fodder for TV sporting-event spectators, historically for the Superbowl but equally appropriate for a Cup Final. To be eaten on site, in front of the telly, with pickles and crisps on the side.

Makes 6-8 sandwiches

1 cup = 225ml (8fl oz)

2 tablespoons fat or dripping
450g (1lb) minced beef
1 onion, chopped
55g (2oz/½ cup) celery, finely chopped
half green pepper, seeded, finely chopped
1 garlic clove, crushed (optional)
50ml (2fl oz/¼ cup) chilli sauce
50ml (2fl oz/½ cup) tomato ketchup
225ml (8fl oz/1 cup) water
1 teaspoon salt
¼ teaspoon freshly ground black pepper
1 tablespoon Worcestershire sauce
2 tablespoons vinegar
2 tablespoons soft brown sugar
1 tablespoon dry mustard
½ tablespoon paprika
1 tablespoon chopped fresh parsley

1. Heat the fat or dripping in a pan, add the minced beef and onion and cook until the mince is browned all over, stirring occasionally. Pour off and discard any excess fat.

2. Add all the remaining ingredients and mix well. Bring to the boil, then reduce the heat, cover and simmer for 45 minutes. By this stage, the mixture should be 'sloppy' but not too wet. If necessary, boil the mixture rapidly until some of the liquid has evaporated, to achieve the correct consistency.

3. Serve on hamburger buns or baps.

Contributed by CAROLINE HAMBURGER

Previous page:
Manager Eddie Keegan tackles a rib of beef that has been aged.

Best stir-fried steak *with horseradish & mustard*

Serves 1

1 tablespoon sunflower oil
350g (12oz) sirloin steak, cut into thin strips
1 tablespoon horseradish sauce
1 teaspoon English mustard
125ml (4fl oz) beef stock
Salt and freshly ground black pepper
Crème fraiche or double cream, to serve

1. Heat the oil in a wok or frying pan, add the steak and stir-fry for about 3–5 minutes, or until just cooked and tender.

2. Add the horseradish sauce and mustard and stir-fry for 30 seconds.

3. Add the stock and seasoning, bring to the boil, then stir in a little crème fraiche or cream and heat until hot (but not boiling). Serve immediately.

Contributed by STELLA FRY

Californian baked beans

Serves 4

1 tablespoon sunflower oil
350g (12oz) lean minced beef
420g can flageolet beans, rinsed and drained
420g can cannellini beans, rinsed and drained
400g can chopped tomatoes
227g can chopped tomatoes
100g (3½oz) demerara sugar
4 onions, very thinly sliced
115g (4oz) streaky bacon rashers

1. Preheat the oven to 170°C/325°F/Gas Mark 3. Heat the oil in a large frying pan, add the minced beef and cook until browned all over, stirring occasionally. Stir in the canned beans and tomatoes and cook for 5 minutes.

2. Spoon half the mixture into an ovenproof casserole dish, sprinkle with half the sugar and cover with the onions.

3. Top with the remaining mince and bean mixture, then arrange the bacon rashers on top. Sprinkle rest of sugar over the bacon.

4. Bake in the oven for 1–1½ hours or until cooked. Serve with braised red cabbage and baked potatoes.

Contributed by FRANCES BROWN

Rosie's tasty beef stew

This recipe is great for a large hungry crowd, preferably in winter (it's hearty), possibly after a chilly outing such as horse-racing or a walk on the Heath. I've often made it for 12 people, even for three dozen for a Christmas party. It can be made and completely finished ahead of time and then reheated. Serve with only lots of good warmed bread and a vast salad, with (bought) dessert to follow. Easy, good food.

Serves 6

1.3kg (3lb) lean stewing beef, cut into cubes
seasoned plain flour
2–3 tablespoons vegetable oil
1 tablespoon salt
1 large onion, minced
1½ garlic cloves, crushed
2 small cans (each about 142g) tomato purée
3 whole cloves
1 bay leaf
13 peppercorns
15g (½oz) chopped fresh parsley
850ml (1½ pints/4 cups) good quality beef stock
6 potatoes, cut into large pieces
6 carrots, cut into large pieces
6 sticks celery, cut into large pieces
225ml (8fl oz/1 cup) sherry

1. Toss the meat in seasoned flour until coated all over, shaking off any excess flour. Heat the oil in a large flameproof, ovenproof casserole dish, add the meat and cook until browned all over, stirring occasionally. Sprinkle with the salt.

2. Meanwhile, in a separate pan, combine the onion, garlic, tomato puree, cloves, bay leaf, peppercorns, parsley and stock and bring to the boil.

3. Pour this mixture over the meat and bring to the boil, stirring. Reduce the heat, cover and simmer for 2 hours, stirring occasionally.

4. Preheat the oven to 180°C/350°F/Gas Mark 4. Add the potatoes, carrots and celery to the casserole and stir to mix. Cover and bake in the oven for 45–60 minutes, or until the meat and vegetables are cooked and tender.

5. Discard the bay leaf and cloves. Stir in the sherry just before serving and reheat gently. Serve.

Contributed by CAROLINE HAMBURGER

Beef meatballs

This is a Finnish family recipe.

Serves 4-6

150ml (¼ pint) fresh breadcrumbs
(about 40g/1½oz)
150ml (¼ pint) double cream
150ml (¼ pint) water
800g (1¾lb) good quality minced beef
2 medium eggs, lightly beaten
4 medium potatoes, boiled,
cooled and grated
2 small onions, grated
½ teaspoon ground allspice
4 teaspoons salt
½ teaspoon white pepper
butter, for frying

1. In a bowl, mix together the breadcrumbs, cream and water. Leave to stand for about 30 minutes.

2. In a large bowl, mix the minced beef with the eggs, then add the breadcrumb mixture, potatoes, onions, allspice and salt and pepper and stir until thoroughly mixed.

3. Shape the mixture into small balls. Melt some butter in a frying pan, add the meatballs and fry, in batches if necessary, for about 15–20 minutes, or until evenly browned all over and cooked right through, turning occasionally.

4. Serve hot or cold with cranberry sauce.

Contributed by MONICA PREBBLE

lamb recipes

Rena Salaman is Greek. She was born and brought up in Athens and was introduced to the culinary pleasures of the world at an early age. She and her husband spend their summers in the family home on the Aegean island of Alonnisos.

Rena has written a number of cookery books on Greek and Mediterranean food, including *Mediterranean Vegetable Cooking*, *Greek Island Cookery*, *Healthy Mediterranean Cooking* and *The Greek Cook*.

Arnaki fricassee *lamb and cos lettuce casserole*

This is a classic spring dish in Greece, particularly during the period following Easter when young lambs are at their best and huge cos lettuces and feathery bunches of fresh dill are found in open-air street markets. This is the best way to cook lamb.

For a special occasion, I use a leg of lamb which is boned and the meat sliced into individual portions. Steele's in Hampstead always have the most delicious tasting lamb and, of course, they always bone and slice the meat expertly for me.

Serve it with a large green salad and some boiled new potatoes and fresh bread — imperative for the delicious sauce.

Previous page:
Two French-trimmed racks of lamb make a Guard of Honour.

Arnaki fricassee *continued*

Serves 6

For the lamb & lettuce casserole
2–3 tablespoons olive oil
1 onion, chopped
1.5kg (3lb 5oz) leg of lamb, boned and
sliced into individual steaks
juice of half lemon
Salt, to taste
2–3 cos lettuces, rinsed, drained and
coarsely shredded
4–5 spring onions, trimmed, rinsed and
coarsely sliced
3 tablespoons coarsely chopped fresh dill

For the egg & lemon sauce
2 medium eggs
1 tablespoon cornflour, blended with
125ml (4fl oz) cold water
juice of 1 lemon

1. Make the casserole. Heat the oil in a large, heavy-based saucepan, add the onion and sauté until glistening.

2. Increase the heat, add the lamb and sauté, stirring, until all its moisture evaporates — about 15 minutes. Add the lemon juice, salt to taste and enough hot water to cover the meat, then cover the pan and simmer for about 1 hour, or until the meat is tender. Take care not to overcook the lamb at this stage.

3. Add the lettuce, spring onions, chopped dill and a little more hot water to cover them, then cover and simmer for a further 15 minutes. Remove the pan from the heat and let the dish stand a little before adding the lemon sauce.

4. Make the lemon sauce. Beat the eggs lightly in a bowl, add the blended cornflour mixture and beat until smooth. Beat in the lemon juice.

5. Gradually add the lemon egg sauce to the meat, stirring continuously, until it looks amalgamated. Return the pan to a gentle heat and cook just enough to warm the sauce through and thicken it, without allowing the sauce to boil, as this may cause the eggs to cook and scramble. Serve.

Contributed by RENA SALAMAN

Lamb roasted *with apples and cider*

Serves 6

1 boned shoulder of lamb (1.3kg/3lb)
pared rind and juice of 1 lemon
450g (1lb) cooking apples, peeled,
cored and sliced
2 tablespoons brown sugar
3 whole cloves
2 teaspoons ground ginger
salt and freshly ground black pepper
2 tablespoons melted dripping or
vegetable oil
450ml (16fl oz/2 cups) cider or apple juice

1. Preheat the oven to 180°C/350°F/Gas Mark 4. Rub the lamb inside and out with the lemon rind and juice. Arrange the apple slices over the inside of the meat and sprinkle with the sugar and cloves.

2. Roll the meat into a roll and secure with skewers or sew up with ovenproof thread.

3. Rub the outside of the meat with a mixture of ginger and salt and pepper, then brush all over with melted dripping or oil. Weigh the stuffed joint and calculate the cooking time, allowing about 25 minutes per 450g (1lb), plus 25 minutes.

4. Place the lamb in a roasting tin and pour over the cider or apple juice. Roast in the oven for the calculated time, basting with cider or apple juice every 15 minutes or so.

5. When the lamb is cooked, drain off the juices from the tin, remove and discard the fat, then rapidly boil the juices in a pan until reduced by about half. Carve the lamb and serve with the sauce.

Contributed by SUSAN LE QUESNE

Lamb with dried apricots

Moroccan-style lamb with a mild spicy flavour. Here's another
J. A. Steele favourite, cooked on top of the stove on a low heat.

Serves 6

boned shoulder of lamb, with the fat cut off
1 packet dried apricots
1 onion
1 litre (2 pints) boiling water
1 teaspoon cumin
1 teaspoon coriander
½ teaspoon allspice
salt and freshly ground black pepper
2 teaspoons olive oil

1. Soak the apricots in the boiling water overnight.

2. Slice the onion thinly and cook on a low heat until pearly white. Place in a saucer to one side.

3. Dice the lamb into 3cm (1inch) cubes. Turn up the heat and sear the meat, moving it around the heavy-bottomed pan quickly to seal it. Return the onions to the pan, add the spices and the soaked apricots. You can add the water from the apricots or use fresh water. Make sure the meat and apricots combined are covered in water. Season to taste.

3. Cook on a low heat for 1½–2 hours. Serve with sliced French bread, and a fresh green salad.

Contributed by LYNN BRYAN

Marinated lamb fillets *with Cumin*

Serves 6

6 small lamb neck fillets
2 medium onions
powdered cumin
salt and freshly ground black pepper
4 tablespoons lemon juice
4 tablespoons olive oil
½ pint sour cream

1. Put the lemon juice and 2 tablespoons of olive oil in a roasting pan. Add the lamb fillets, sprinkled on both sides with pepper, and turn them back and forth in the mixture. Leave in a cool place, covered with foil, overnight. Turn the fillets over every now and then, and spoon the mixture over them.

2. When marinated to your satisfaction, pour off the surplus mixture. Sprinkle the fillets generously with the powdered cumin. Heat some of the oil in a heavy frying pan and add the fillets. Cook them slowly, turning several times, for about 20 minutes. Transfer them to a serving dish and keep warm.

3. Slice the onions in rings as finely as possible. Fry them gently in the juices remaining in the pan until transparent but not too soft. Arrange onions on top of the fillets.

4. Heat the sour cream in the remaining juices to nearly boiling point. Pour the sour cream over the fillets and onions. Serve with small new potatoes and crisp green beans.

Note: When the lamb is marinated for long enough, it will melt in your mouth. Buy English or Welsh lamb when in season because it is so much better.

Contributed by MRS AKIN

Meat terrine

Serves 4-6

225g (8oz) lamb's liver
450g (1lb) minced pork
225g (8oz) sausage meat
175g (6oz) streaky bacon
1 onion, chopped
2 medium eggs
1 tablespoon chopped fresh mixed herbs
55g (2oz) fresh breadcrumbs
pinch of ground mace
salt and freshly ground black pepper
1 bay leaf

1. Preheat the oven to 170°C/325°F/Gas Mark 3. Lightly grease a loaf tin or terrine dish (about 1.3kg/3lb in size) and set aside. Place all the ingredients, except the bay leaf, in a blender or food processor and blend until finely chopped and well mixed.

2. Transfer the mixture to the prepared loaf tin and level the surface. Place the bay leaf on top and cover with foil. Bake in the oven for 1–1½ hours, or until cooked.

3. Turn out onto a serving plate. Serve hot or cold in slices, with a fresh tomato sauce.

Contributed by J. READ

pork
recipes

LAMB
mint
£3.80

Pork
+
leek
£2.80

An actor's tale

(I enter the shop.)

JS: "How's the best-looking young man in Hampstead?"

PB: "Fine, thanks. I'd like – er….."

JS: (to another customer who's just come in) "Good morning madam, you are the most charming lady. Do you know the best-looking young actor in Hampstead?"

Customer: "Er……."

Eddie: "He's even been in some films in colour."

Barry: "Yes. Mostly black and white though."

PB: "I'd like some spare rib chops, please. Two. Not too big."

Barry: "We'll cut them especially for you."

JS: "Special for the most charming man in Hampstead. See to it, Barry. Make a fuss of him." (He disappears up the most – er – amazing staircase in Hampstead.)

Barry: (showing the two chops he's just cut): "Special".

PB: "How much?"

Barry: "One eighty-two".

PB: "Cheap. It always amazes me: things can be cheap here."

Barry: "Thank-you sir."

(I leave the shop.)

Eddie: "Mind the step".

(Back home, I prepare the evening's supper).

Actor's pork and apple

Serves 2-4

1 spare-rib pork chop, per person
mustard (of your choice), for spreading
enough peeled, cored and sliced eating
apples to cover each chop
small dollop of marmalade, per chop

1. Preheat the oven to 170°C/325°F/Gas Mark 3. Cut the bone and any surplus fat from the chops, then place them side-by-side in an ovenproof casserole dish.

2. On top of each chop, spread a little mustard, then arrange the apple slices over the mustard. Top each chop with a small dollop of marmalade.

3. Put the lid on the casserole and bake in the oven for about 2 hours, or until the chops are cooked and tender. Serve with …..Oh…..what you like.

Cook's Tip

I prefer to cook these chops at 150°C/300°F/Gas Mark 2 for about 3 hours, if there is time.

Contributed by PETER BARKWORTH

Baked crusted gammon

This recipe has been a firm favourite in our family for generations. It was handed down to me by my late mother-in-law, Mrs. Dorothy Dean, formerly of Gayton Road, who produced this succulent ham every Christmas, every Easter and for any special occasion.

Serves 6-8

12 prunes
1 gammon joint, about 1.3–1.8kg (3–4lb)
850ml (1½ pints) apple cider vinegar
1 large egg
225g (8oz) soft brown sugar
1 tablespoon dry mustard

1. Soak the prunes and the gammon for a minimum of 24 hours (36 hours, preferably) in cold water or, when feeling lavish, replace the water with 50% rough cider.

2. Drain the gammon and prunes and place in a large pan. Add enough water (or water and cider mixture) to almost cover, then add about 600ml (1 pint) of the vinegar.

3. Bring to the boil, then reduce the heat and simmer for the calculated time, allowing 20 minutes for each 450g (1lb).

4. Preheat the oven to 200°C/400°F/Gas Mark 6. Lift the gammon out of the pan, cool sufficiently to handle, remove the skin (but not the fat) and place in a dry baking tin.

5. Mix the egg, sugar and mustard together in a basin. Coat the gammon with this paste. Pour the remaining vinegar around the gammon and bake in the oven for 50 minutes, basting every 15 minutes. Carve into slices and serve.

Cook's Tip

When soaking gammon, change the water periodically, say every 12 hours, and add the rough cider at the last change for a final 12 hours. This helps remove the salt from the meat more quickly.

Contributed by JANE DEAN

Fillet of pork

Serves 2-4

1 piece of pork fillet
red wine, for marinating
crushed juniper berries, for marinating
dripping, for frying
plain flour, for roux sauce
pork or chicken stock, for sauce
chopped fresh mixed herbs, to garnish

1. In a non-metallic dish, marinade a piece of pork fillet in red wine and crushed juniper berries in a cool place for 12 hours.

2. Slice the pork thinly and obliquely into medallions. Pan-fry slowly in dripping. Remove when cooked and lightly browned. Keep warm.

3. Add a little flour to the pan and stir to make a roux. Cook gently for 1 minute, stirring, then gradually stir in a small amount of stock and the marinade, until you have the sort of thickness that you prefer for your sauce. Heat until hot and bubbling, stirring.

4. Serve the pork with the sauce poured over. Garnish with chopped herbs and serve with a good claret.

Contributed by PROFESSOR MICHAEL & DR. MICKY DAY

Fried gammon steak

Being now incredibly old and unable to lift a roasting tin or even a casserole from the oven, I am obliged to rely on the grill and frying pan. Here is the first of two recipes I contrive.

Serves 1

sunflower oil, for frying
1 gammon steak
plenty of fresh mint sauce, to serve

1. Heat a little oil in a frying pan, add the gammon steak and fry for about 10–15 minutes, or until thoroughly cooked, turning once.

2. Serve with cooked new potatoes, broad beans and peas and plenty of mint sauce.

Contributed by MARY EPSTEIN

Mom's ham loaf

Serves 6-8

For the ham loaf
450g (1lb) mixed minced ham and pork
about 5 tablespoons fresh breadcrumbs
2 medium eggs, lightly beaten
1 teaspoon minced onion
1 can (295g) condensed tomato soup
salt and freshly ground black pepper

For the glaze
350g (12oz/1½ cups) soft brown sugar
125ml (4fl oz/½ cup) water
125ml (4fl oz/½ cup) vinegar
2 teaspoons French mustard
8 whole cloves

For the sauce
3 tablespoons mayonnaise
125ml (4fl oz/½ cup) double or whipping cream, whipped
1 tablespoon vinegar
2 tablespoons grated fresh (peeled) horseradish (or horseradish sauce)
1 teaspoon French mustard
½ teaspoon salt
pinch of cayenne pepper

In the American Midwest, a 'loaf' made with various meats is a main meal classic. If this recipe is used for entertaining, the guests must be good friends, and the ham loaf must be consumed at the kitchen table.

1. Preheat the oven to 200°C/400°F/Gas Mark 6. Lightly grease a loaf tin (about 900g/2lb in size) and set aside. Make the ham loaf. Place all the loaf ingredients in a bowl and mix together thoroughly, adding enough breadcrumbs to make a stiff mixture.

2. Transfer the mixture to the prepared loaf tin and level the surface. Set aside. Make the glaze. Place all the glaze ingredients in a pan, bring to the boil, stirring, then boil for 8 minutes.

3. Pour the glaze over the ham loaf. Bake, uncovered, in the oven for 45 minutes. Reduce the temperature to 170°C/325°F/Gas Mark 3, cover the loaf and bake for a further 1 hour.

4. Meanwhile, make the sauce. Fold the mayonnaise into the whipped cream, then gradually fold in the vinegar. Add all the remaining ingredients and fold in gently to mix. Chill in the refrigerator until ready to serve.

5. Turn the cooked ham loaf out onto a plate and serve in slices with the sauce alongside.

Contributed by CAROLINE HAMBURGER

Mustard-grilled pork chop

Serves 1

1 pork chop
1–2 teaspoons olive oil
1–2 tablespoons Dijon mustard
(or mustard of your choice)
1 tablespoon brown sugar
apple sauce
1 teaspoon fresh sage, chopped

1. Preheat the grill to medium. Trim the pork chop and brush olive oil over both sides.

2. Spread each side of the chop quite thickly with some mustard and sprinkle a little brown sugar over the top, pressing it down lightly.

3. Place on a grill rack and cook under the grill for about 15–20 minutes, or until thoroughly cooked, turning once.

4. Fold 1 teaspoon chopped fresh sage into the apple sauce. Serve hot with apple sauce and your choice of vegetables.

Contributed by MARY EPSTEIN

veal
recipes

Osso buco alla romana Braised shin of veal

Osso buco are slices of a shin of veal which are braised slowly until they are meltingly sweet. Originally a Milanese dish — 'bone with a hole'— it contained tomatoes and was traditionally served with Risotto alla Milanese (saffron and bone marrow risotto), with a Gremolata (a mixture of grated lemon zest and chopped garlic and parsley) sprinkled on top.

The first time I had osso buco was in a small restaurant in Rome, under the shade of the Vatican and it was different from what I had expected. It was the purest version and is the only way I have cooked it since. Serve with sautéed potatoes and spinach.

Serves 4

3 tablespoons olive oil
4 pieces of osso buco, 1.1kg (2lb 6oz) in weight (each 2.5cm/1in thick)
2 tablespoons plain flour
4–5 fresh sage leaves
150ml (¼ pint) dry white wine
425ml (¾ pint) hot chicken stock or water
2 long pieces of fresh or dried orange peel (from an unwaxed orange)
salt and freshly ground black pepper
5–6 fresh basil leaves, rinsed, torn into pieces

1. Use a large, heavy-based sauté pan or flameproof casserole dish which will take the osso buco in a single layer. Heat the oil in the pan. Pat the meat dry and coat lightly in flour, shaking off any excess flour. When the oil is hot, add the meat and brown it quickly on both sides. It should be lightly golden in colour.

2. Then, add the sage leaves. A minute later, pour the wine over. Let it sizzle and evaporate for a few minutes, then add the stock or water, the orange peel and salt and pepper. Cover and simmer for 1½ hours or until the meat is very soft. Turn the pieces of meat over a couple of times during cooking, but be careful not to split the marrow from its centre.

3. When cooked, sprinkle the torn basil leaves over the top. Cover and simmer for a few more minutes. By now, the sauce will be thick, velvety and full of aromas. Serve.

Contributed by RENA SALAMAN

Roast fillet of veal

For a delicious Sunday lunch party

Serves 6

2kg/4½lbs fillet of veal
8 quartered red tomatoes
10 whole new potatoes, peeled
2 cloves garlic, sliced
½ bottle dry white wine
½ cup chicken stock
1 tablespoon olive oil
142 ml (about ¼ pint) carton double cream

1. Sear the meat in a hot non-stick roasting pan with a little olive oil until golden brown on all sides.

2. Add the quartered tomatoes. whole new potatoes and slices of garlic.

3. Mix the white wine with the chicken stock and add slowly to the pan. Mix well to include all the sticky bits at the bottom of the pan, coating the meat as well. Bring to the boil and simmer for five minutes.

4. Transfer to a hot oven (170°C/325°F/Gas Mark 3) and cook for 1 hour and 10 minutes. Baste every 10 minutes to keep the meat moist.

5. When the meat is cooked, remove from the pan and place on a serving plate. Place the roasting pan with juices back on a low-heat hob and add the double cream to make a gravy. Do not boil. When the gravy is ready, pour into a sauce boat and serve.

Contributed by JUDY GREEN

Veal escalopes *with asparagus & balsamic vinegar*

From *The New Penguin Cookery Book*

Serves 4

400g (14oz) veal escalopes
300g (10½oz) green asparagus
2 tablespoons olive oil
40g (1½oz) butter
150ml (¼ pint) white wine
salt and freshly ground black pepper
4 teaspoons balsamic vinegar

1. Flatten the veal escalopes gently. Break the asparagus to give pieces 8–10cm (3–4in) long and use the rest of the stalks for soup. Thread the spears carefully onto thin wooden skewers. Preheat the grill or a ribbed griddle plate.

2. Put 1 tablespoon oil and 25g (1oz) butter into a frying pan and place over a medium heat. When the fat is hot, fry the escalopes for 3 minutes each side, turning once, until lightly browned. When they are ready, remove them to a plate and keep warm.

3. Meanwhile, brush the asparagus with the remaining oil and put them under the grill or on the griddle plate. Grill for 4–5 minutes, depending on thickness, turning once.

4. When all the escalopes are cooked, add the wine to the pan and scrape up any bits stuck to the bottom. Let the wine bubble until it is reduced to only a couple of tablespoons, then add remaining butter and any juices from the escalopes.

5. Season the meat and return to the pan. Turn the pieces a few times in the pan juices, then add 3 teaspoons balsamic vinegar and turn the meat once more. Transfer the escalopes and juices to a serving dish, remove the asparagus from the skewers and lay across the meat.

6. Drizzle the last teaspoon of balsamic vinegar over the asparagus and serve at once.

Contributed by JILL NORMAN

chicken and poultry recipes

Aussie apricot chicken

This is my Australian au pair's mother's recipe. This is a real quickie for a day spent shopping in Hampstead, when you want the family or guests to think you've actually spent time cooking (yet you haven't). It's amazingly impressive and gloriously easy. Truly a capolavoro, masterpiece, of the Aussie 'no worries' school of cooking.

Serves 4

2 tablespoons vegetable oil
4 chicken portions
400g can apricots in fruit juice, puréed
1 can (about 295g) condensed onion soup

1. Preheat the oven to 170°C/325°F/Gas Mark 3. Heat the oil in a flameproof, ovenproof casserole dish. Add the chicken and cook until browned all over, turning occasionally.

2. Mix the puréed apricots and onion soup together and pour over the chicken. Cover and cook in the oven for about 1 hour, or until the chicken is cooked and tender. Serve.

Contributed by CAROLINE HAMBURGER

Barbecue chicken

Summer in Hampstead is a beautiful time, especially in August when the roads are empty. We always look forward to at least one Saturday night at Kenwood when, armed with a picnic and copious amounts of wine, we settle down to an evening of music and fireworks under the stars. Every year's the same…. moaning while carrying over-filled bags on the way there, and staggering back across the Heath in darkness after.

Barbecue chicken *continued*

We once introduced a young Canadian couple to the delights of Kenwood — they were amazed alcohol was permitted as it is prohibited at outdoor events in Toronto. They were even more amazed when someone came round offering free samples of gin and tonic!

No picnic is complete without these barbecue chicken legs … sweet, sticky and great for eating with your fingers. I was given this recipe thirty years ago in Canada and every year when I make them, it heralds the start of summer and the picnic season.

Makes 12 drumsticks

For the chicken
12 chicken portions (I use drumsticks)
115g (4oz) plain flour, seasoned with crushed garlic and paprika

For the sauce
half bottle tomato ketchup
6 tablespoons soft brown sugar
1 teaspoon soy sauce
1 teaspoon mustard (of your choice)
1 teaspoon vinegar
1 teaspoon Worcestershire sauce

1. Preheat the oven to 170°C/325°F/Gas Mark 3. Lightly grease a baking sheet and set aside. Prepare the chicken. Dip the chicken portions in the seasoned flour, until lightly coated all over. Shake off any excess flour.

2. Arrange the chicken portions on the prepared baking sheet and bake in the oven for 30 minutes.

3. Meanwhile, make the sauce. Place all the sauce ingredients in a bowl and mix together well.

4. Dip each piece of hot chicken into the sauce to coat all over. Return to the baking sheet and cook in the oven for a further 30 minutes, or until the chicken is cooked and tender.

5. Remove from the oven and allow to cool. Eat cold, making sure you bring plenty of kitchen paper or wet cloths for sticky hands.

Contributed by VICKI (Well Walk)

Best roast chicken of all

The secret of this recipe is long, slow cooking, so everything caramelises.

Serves 4-6

Honey, for spreading
mustard (of your choice), for spreading
1 free-range oven-ready chicken, weighing about 1.5kg (3lb 5oz)
3–4 tablespoons olive oil
lots of garlic cloves (great big cloves), peeled
2–3 onions, sliced
3–4 carrots, sliced
2–3 tablespoons chopped fresh tarragon
salt and freshly ground black pepper
Balsamic vinegar, to taste

1. Preheat the oven to 170°C/325°F/Gas Mark 3. Spread some honey and mustard over the whole chicken. Set aside.

2. Heat the oil in a large, flameproof, ovenproof casserole dish. Add the garlic and onions and sauté until browned all over. Remove them to a plate and set aside.

3. Add the chicken to the pan and cook until browned all over, turning occasionally. Add the carrots, tarragon and seasoning, plus the garlic and onions, then splash some balsamic vinegar over the lot.

4. Add about 225ml (8fl oz) water to stop it sticking, then cover, shove the dish in the oven and cook for about 2–2½ hours, or until the chicken is cooked and tender, removing the lid for the last 30 minutes or so. The sauce should be deliciously tacky. Leave to stand for 10 minutes or so, before carving and serving, to release the flavours.

Contributed by DEBORAH MOGGACH

Butcher's paella

This is a quick and easy recipe made by Barry Steele when he arrives home from a day at Flask Walk. He swears it is delicious and hopes your enjoyment of it will sell more chorizo sausages!

Serves 4-6

1 teaspoon vegetable oil

400g (14oz) chorizo sausages cut in 10mm (½ in) diagonal slices

1 small red onion, chopped

1 red pepper, chopped

2 cloves of garlic, chopped

¼ teaspoon paprika

2 cups rice

pinch saffron

2 bay leaves

4 cups (16fl oz) chicken stock

560g/1¼lb roast chicken from a 1.5kg (3lb) bird, torn into chunks

half a cup of frozen peas

1 tomato, chopped

salt and pepper to taste

1. Preheat the oven to 200°C/400°F/Gas Mark 6. Heat the oil in a large casserole dish over high heat. Add the chorizo sausages. Cook until browned and fragrant (1 minute).

2. Add the onion, red pepper and garlic. Cook, stirring occasionally until vegetables are tender (3 minutes).

3. Add the rice, paprika, saffron and bay leaves. Stir to combine with the rice (1 minute).

4. Add the chicken stock. Bring to the boil.

5. Add the roast chicken pieces, frozen peas and tomato. Stir to combine.

6. Transfer to the oven and cook uncovered until the rice is tender and no liquid remains — about 20 minutes.

7. Stir through with a fork and then serve.

Contributed by BARRY STEELE

Chicken alla Mama Conti

Mama Conti was actually Scottish. A number of Italians settled there in the Twenties, and began dating the local girls. Sitting around the grappa of an evening, one of the Italians observed, "My Gad! If we are goin' to marryin' dese girls, we are going to starvin' to death! Dey don't cook nottin' at all."

So the Italian men, who from helping their mothers as children knew how to cook, gave the local girls cooking lessons. Life changed for many Scottish in-laws. Fearful at first of "a'that foreign muck", they were quickly converted to the delights of the Italian kitchen — and on the evening table, the wine bottle displaced the teapot. This dish, one of the first to be taught, is simple to make.

Serves 4-6

2 large onions, sliced
olive oil, for coating
1 oven-ready chicken, about 1.5kg (3lb 5oz)
salt, for sprinkling

1. Preheat the oven to 190°C/375°F/Gas Mark 5. Put the onions in a roasting pan and coat them in a liberal helping of oil.

2. Oil the chicken and salt it all over — more than is healthy — and place it on the bed of onions.

3. Allowing 20 minutes per 450g (1lb) chicken, plus 20 minutes, roast the chicken in the oven for the calculated time. Turn up the heat for the last 15 minutes, so that the onions burn somewhat and the chicken skin becomes crispy.

4. Tip the 'schmaltz' (a word from the Jewish kitchen) out of the bird and mix it with the onion juices. Heat in a pan until hot. This becomes a wonderful sauce in which to fold the chicken slices.

5. Carve the chicken into slices and serve with the sauce. Fried red peppers and roast parsnips go pretty well with this — as does a good Pouilly Fumé. *Buon divertimento.*

Contributed by TOM CONTI

Chicken sauté with garlic

This recipe comes from a *Time Life* Cookery Book and they in turn attribute it to *A Table Avec Edouard Pomiane* by Ginette Mathiot.

This is a flexible dish and quantities and cuts of chicken can be varied easily according to the number of servings required and preferences for leg, breast, etc. I always use chicken supremes, although the recipe states a whole chicken, cut into pieces.

Serves 4-6

40g (1½oz) butter
4 tablespoons olive oil
1.3–1.8kg (3–4lb) oven-ready chicken, cut into pieces (jointed)
30 garlic cloves, unpeeled
10 shallots, finely chopped
salt and freshly ground black pepper
150ml (¼ pint) dry white wine

1. Heat the butter and oil in a sauté pan or cast-iron casserole dish. Place the chicken pieces in the pan and brown them lightly on one side over a medium heat, to avoid burning the fat. Turn the chicken pieces over and brown them lightly on the other side.

2. Add the garlic cloves and shallots. Sauté for 10 minutes or until the skin of the garlic is lightly coloured.

3. Season liberally with salt and pepper, then add the wine. Cover the pan and cook gently for about 30 minutes or until all the wine has evaporated.

4. Take the pan to the table and serve the chicken pieces with the garlic cloves. Eat the garlic with the chicken; bite into each clove and remove the tough skin to your plate. The taste is exquisite.

Contributed by TIM LORD

Barbary duck, roasted *a la confiture d'orange*

Serves 4-5

1 large whole fresh Barbary duck
salt and freshly ground black pepper
5 garlic cloves, crushed, plus a few extra
garlic cloves left whole
good-quality orange marmalade

1. Preheat the oven to 200°C/400°F/Gas Mark 6. Clean the duck. Prick the skin with a sharp serving fork, especially around the fatty parts such as near the neck and between the thighs and breast (this will cause the fat between the skin and the meat to drip out during cooking). Rub the skin and the inside cavity with salt, pepper and crushed garlic. Place a few whole garlic cloves in the cavity.

2. Spread a thick coat of marmalade evenly over the skin. Place in a roasting tin and bake for 30 minutes. The skin will look quite dark early in the cooking process because of the marmalade which caramelises, but the duck is not yet fully cooked.

3. Reduce the oven temperature to 180°C/350°F/Gas Mark 4 and continue roasting the duck for a further 20–30 minutes, or until cooked and tender. Remove from the oven and rest for 10 minutes before serving. Carve at the table. If you believe the French, you will want the tail (or botty), which, to some, is the best part of the bird! Serve with gravy, vegetables and apple sauce.

To make gravy

Remove the roasting tin from the oven and discard the liquid fat from the tin. Save and collect all the dark residue in a pan, add half a glass of chicken, duck or vegetable stock, together with a squirt of orange juice and a drop of Grand Marnier. Mix well.

Contributed by HORACIO FURMAN

Colombian *Ajiaco*

Serves 6-8

2kg (4lb) free-range or organic chicken
2 large onions, peeled and quartered
a handful of coriander sprigs
3 litres (6 pints) water
1kg (2lbs) soft-cooking potatoes, peeled and thickly sliced
1kg (2 lbs) firm potatoes, peeled and sliced
500g (1lb) small waxy salad potatoes, scrubbed and halved, or left whole if small
bunch of watercress, leaves only
3 or 4 sweetcorn
fresh green or red chilli, or crushed dried chillies to taste
salt to taste
fresh coriander

1. Rinse and dry the chicken, and remove any cavity fat. Put it in a large saucepan with the onion, coriander stalks and water to cover the chicken. Bring to the boil, remove any scum from the surface, cover, and simmer gently for 15 minutes.

2. Add the soft-cooking potatoes, and cook for a further 25 to 30 minutes. Remove the coriander and onion and discard. Take out the chicken, and put to one side.

3. Put in the rest of the potatoes, and cook for 15 to 20 minutes until the first batch is quite soft enough for you to break up with a fork and the other two kinds of potato are still firm but cooked.

4. Meanwhile, remove the meat from the chicken carcass. Add the chilli and watercress to the pan with the corn, each cut into three or four pieces, and bring to the boil. Put in the chicken meat, and simmer for 5 minutes until the corn is tender. Stir in the coriander, ladle into deep soup bowls, and serve very hot.

5. The traditional accompaniments for ajiaco, served in separate bowls for everyone to help themselves, are: thick yoghurt or cream, capers, chopped parsley and aji (a hot sauce of finely chopped spring onion or leek, tomato, fresh chillies and fresh coriander leaves, mixed with lime juice or vinegar). Each person is also served half an avocado, peeled and sliced on a side plate.

Contributed by FRANCES BISSELL

Easy guinea fowl

This is the easiest dish in the world.

Serves 2

2–3 tablespoons olive oil
1 oven-ready guinea fowl
1 onion
1 orange
1 lemon
225ml (8fl oz) whisky
1–2 carrots, sliced
salt and freshly ground black pepper

1. Preheat the oven to 180°C/350°F/Gas Mark 4. Heat the oil in a heavy flameproof, ovenproof casserole dish. Add the guinea fowl and onion and cook until the bird is browned all over.

2. When the bird is sizzling, slice up the orange and lemon and squeeze the juice over the bird. This will make it sizzle more.

3. Add the whisky, the orange and lemon slices and carrots. Add a little water if necessary, and season with salt and pepper.

4. Cover and cook in the oven for about 1¼–1½ hours, or until the guinea fowl is cooked and tender, removing the lid for the final 15 minutes or so. The gravy should be deliciously tacky. Leave to stand for 10 minutes or so, before serving.

Contributed by DEBORAH MOGGACH

Left:
Weighing up the chicken situation.

Ginger chicken *with leeks*

Serves 2

butter, for greasing
2 chicken breasts, thighs or legs
(skinned, if preferred)
3-4 pieces of preserved stem ginger,
plus a little ginger syrup
2 large or 4 small leeks (white part only),
washed
2 oranges
1 lemon
salt and ground ground pepper (optional)

1. Preheat the oven to 190°C/375°F/Gas Mark 5. Cut 2 large squares of foil, each big enough to comfortably hold one piece of chicken. Lightly grease the foil with a little butter.

2. Place a piece of chicken on each piece of foil. Chop the stem ginger and scatter over the chicken, then drizzle a little ginger syrup over the top. Cut the leeks into julienne strips and scatter evenly over the ginger and chicken.

3. Squeeze the juice from the oranges and lemon and pour it into a small pan. Bring to the boil, boil rapidly for 2 minutes to reduce, then pour over the chicken and leeks. Season to taste with salt and pepper.

4. Fold the top of the foil over the chicken and crimp the edges together to form a tight seal, taking care not to pierce the foil. Place in a baking dish and cook in the oven for about 45–60 minutes, or until the chicken is cooked and tender.

5. Open up the foil parcels and serve the chicken, vegetables and juices on warm serving plates.

Contributed by CLAUDETTE O'KEEFFE

Spiced chicken

This recipe comes with fond memories of the fun times we spent together concocting tasty dishes and devouring them.

Serves 4

8 chicken thighs or drumsticks

juice of 3 lemons or lemon juice

2 teaspoons chilli powder or seasoning

1$\frac{1}{2}$ teaspoons garlic salt

$\frac{1}{2}$ teaspoon ground ginger

$\frac{1}{2}$ teaspoon ground nutmeg

$\frac{1}{4}$ teaspoon ground cinnamon

1$\frac{1}{2}$ teaspoons paprika

1 teaspoon freshly ground black pepper

salt, to taste

2 tablespoons vegetable oil

1. Skin and score the chicken thighs/drumsticks and arrange them in a shallow grill pan. Rub the meaty parts all over with lemon juice.

2. Place all the ground spices and seasonings in a bowl and mix together thoroughly. Scatter the spice mixture over both sides of each of the chicken pieces. Cover and leave overnight in the refrigerator, or for 2–4 hours at room temperature.

3. Preheat the grill to high. Brush one side of the chicken pieces with the oil, then place under the grill for 5 minutes. Turn the chicken pieces over and baste with the oil from the grill pan. Grill for a further 5 minutes.

4. Turn the chicken pieces over and lower the heat to medium. Continue to grill the chicken slowly for 15–30 minutes, turning the chicken pieces once more during this time to ensure both sides are evenly cooked.

5. Serve the chicken pieces with boiled long grain rice and a green salad.

Contributed by GERALDO LONGBOURN and MEG SANCTUS

Walk, flask, chicken

An easy recipe that allows you to combine the pleasures of some of the best things Hampstead has to offer: fine food from a fine butcher, its Heath and its excellent hostelries. In summer, there is only one way to enjoy roast chicken, and that is with rice. The key elements of this dish are the succulent meat from the slow cooking and the gravy flavoured by the giblets.

For the roast chicken
1 oven-ready chicken with giblets, about 1.5kg (3lb 5oz)
1 onion, sliced
fresh thyme sprigs, bay leaves and other woody herbs
2 garlic cloves, left whole
butter, for greasing
salt and freshly ground black pepper
vermouth, white or red wine, or marsala, for deglazing, plus extra stock for the gravy

For the rice
½ onion, per person, chopped
½-1 garlic clove, per person, finely chopped
1 tablespoon olive oil
100ml (3½fl oz) basmati rice, per person
150ml (¼ pint) chicken stock, per person

1. Put the giblets in a saucepan, cover with water, bring to the boil and simmer gently. Preheat the oven to 110°C/225°F/Gas Mark 4.

2. Make a bed for the chicken with the onion and half the herbs in the bottom of a roasting tin. Place the garlic and remaining herbs inside the chicken and tie its legs together. Butter the chicken all over as you would a thick slice of farmhouse bread. Season with salt and pepper. Place the chicken in the roasting tin, then put it into the oven.

3. Place the onion and garlic in a heavy-based saucepan with the oil. Set aside. Place the appropriate quantity of rice in a measuring jug. Fill the kettle. If you haven't bought packets of salad, do any washing/preparing required. Turn off the giblets.

4. You are now ready to go for a walk on Hampstead Heath and/or take in a pint of top quality real ale at such fine hostelries as The Flask or The Duke of Hamilton.

5. You have about 3 hours to enjoy Hampstead. If you need more time, turn the temperature down — no lower than 75°C. If hungry and not very energetic, it will be ready in 2–2¼ hours at

For the salad

selection of green leaves such as rocket, watercress and baby spinach

vinaigrette, to serve

140°C/275°F/Gas Mark 1. The chicken is cooked when the thickest part of its flesh reaches a temperature of 65-70°C. The closer you get to this temperature the more succulent it will be, but in practice there is a good safety margin. Our record is a game of tennis, a walk on the Heath and a pint before feasting on a 75°C bird.

6. When you get home, take the chicken out of the oven and cover with foil. Turn the oven up to 200°C/400°F/Gas Mark 6. When the oven is hot, put the chicken in for 5–10 minutes, to crisp up the skin.

7. Gently fry the onion and garlic until softened, stirring occasionally. Add the rice and stir for a minute. Take the pan off the heat and add the appropriate quantity of stock. Cover, simmer for 10–15 minutes, or until the rice is cooked.

8. When the chicken's skin is done, take it out and put it on a carving dish. Remove the onion and other bits from the roasting tin (we like to leave them in) and place on the hob. Deglaze the pan with alcohol then add the strained stock from the giblets pan. Simmer for a few minutes. Taste and adjust seasoning.

9. While you finish the gravy, someone else can carve the chicken and/or dress the salad. Now eat and enjoy your Walk on the Heath, Flask of beer and roast chicken combo now complete.

Contributed by MARK HARPER, RENATE ERIKSEN, MILDRED & LOUIS

Ye olde Pilgrim poultry stuffing

I stuff this into our Thanksgiving turkey.

Thanksgiving is a little holiday we have on the other side of the pond. It happens on the last Thursday in November and what we're doing is celebrating the Pilgrims Father's first harvest in 1621. These are the people who, having survived an arduous sea voyage over from England, where wars and economic woes and religious persecution were making life unbearable – hoped to establish a new society in the wilderness and give birth to the American Dream (which turns out to be shopping malls, designer outlets, and a Starbucks every six feet, but this wasn't their fault).

The Pilgrim Fathers invited Chief Massasoit, their native American aka Indian (or to be politically correct, Heap Big Redskin) friend and ally to their feast, and he brought along ninety unexpected guest warriors — so how much of a holiday this first Thanksgiving was for the five pilgrim mothers who suddenly had to come up with ninety extra dinners, remains unclear. But could possibly pinpoint the origin of the phrase "FHB" (Family Hold Back).

This stuffing works equally well in a Brit Christmas turkey.

Ye olde Pilgrim poultry stuffing *continued*

225g (8oz/1 cup) butter
450g (1lb) herby sausage meat
1 large onion, finely chopped
2 cloves garlic, finely chopped
4 sticks celery, chopped
2–3 crisp eating apples, peeled, cored and chopped
350g (12oz/2 cups) mixed dried fruit such as ready-to-eat dried apricots, prunes and sultanas, roughly chopped
115g (4oz/1 cup) fresh cranberries
115g (4oz/1 cup) pecans, chopped
55g (2oz/1 cup) chopped fresh parsley
400g (14oz/2 cups) cooked wild rice, cooled
115g (4oz/2 cups) stale bread (not white air bread), cut into small cubes
225ml (8fl oz/1 cup) chicken stock
chopped fresh herbs (sage, marjoram, rosemary), to taste
salt and freshly ground black pepper

Measurements here are approximate guides only. Feel free to wing it.

This recipe makes plenty of stuffing for 1 large Christmas turkey.

1. Melt a little of the butter in a large sauté pan, add the sausage meat, breaking it up into small pieces, and sauté until cooked but not browned. Remove from the pan, drain off and discard any excess fat and set aside.

2. Melt 115g (4oz/$\frac{1}{2}$ cup) butter in the pan, add the onion, garlic and celery and sauté until soft. Set aside.

3. In a large bowl, combine the apples, dried fruit, cranberries, pecan nuts, parsley, rice, bread cubes, sausage meat and onion mixture and mix well.

4. Melt the remaining butter in a small pan, then add the butter to the stuffing mixture, together with as much stock as needed to moisten the stuffing. Add chopped herbs and salt and pepper, to taste.

5. Stuff the bird, realise you've made a ton more than you need, wrap the excess stuffing in a foil packet and roast it separately, opening the foil towards the end of the cooking time, to crisp it. Or, put the excess stuffing in the freezer, forget about it, and throw it away when you find it two years later.

Contributed by ASTRID KING

Turkey, turkey, burning bright

The last Thursday in November is a big day for Patriotic Yanks Overseas: Thanksgiving. Basically, it involves cooking up a storm and then eating ourselves sick. Oh, and a big turkey.

Trouble is, Brit kitchen appliances are teeny, and you can't jam a big turkey into these ovens unless a) you break its legs and/or b) pound the handles off your Yank-size roasting pans.

The obvious solution — not counting getting an invite to someone else's house, or going with quail — is, of course, the barbecue. But this can be kinda tricky, even if you've installed your Webber (those covered kettle-drum kind) four flights up on a roof terrace. So pay attention, haul out your foul-weather gear, and file the following under Recipes for Disaster:

One month before Secure in the knowledge that Americans are born to Bar-B-Q (it's in our jeans), invite everyone under the sun (that hot yellow thing in the sky you used to see before you moved here), order a 28-pound turkey from Steele's, and make your mother in Massachusetts who's sick of mailing things, send Pilgrim hats, gourds, and Indian corn. If she says "You can't get napkins in Britain?", tell her "Yes, but not with turkeys on them" (and not for free).

One week before Divest London of canned pumpkin, Karo syrup, etc., work out a timetable for 900 vegetable dishes, and bake turkey-shaped sugar cookie place-cards with multi-coloured icing feathers and red gobbles. (For Halloween, I do bats, for Easter, I do bunnies and flags for 4th July. Not sure yet re: Guy Fawkes or Bank Holiday Monday, but will keep you posted).

T-Day minus two Finish maple syrup ice cream with pecan praline, gingered pear pickles, clam dip, and shop for autumnal-shaped salt cellars and fake leaves from France on which to serve cheese. And other last minute essentials.

Less than 24 hours to go Discover you're out of charcoal and that London's not overflowing with it in late November. Tear home, ring everyone you know to check garden sheds, instruct Brit husband to check every gas station on way home from work, and live for news like "I can get you half a bag from a mother at school, she says it's a little damp, though."

Around midnight While counting briquettes, start wondering how big a 28-pound turkey is, and what you do if it turns out to be bigger than the barbecue (with the oven full of those well-planned 900 vegetable dishes).

The Big Day Wake, sweating, throw off nightgown and race to butcher's (dressing first). Stare, concerned, at ostrich-sized item being held up for inspection. Remember reading the term 'Laid Back Turkey' somewhere. Say, slowly, "Could you maybe take the backbone out of this sucker?" Mr. Steele will say 'For you, young lady? Anything. You're gorgeous'. (Brit butchers go to charm school. They can gut, fillet and remove hind quarters, while simultaneously suckering female customers wearing whatever the cat dragged in, into believing they're hotter than Rita Hayworth. For an instant lift, move to England and buy meat from a butcher).

Turkey, turkey, burning bright continued

The turkey, spineless, will appear larger, draped down all four sides of the butchers block, and it will look like a road accident. Lug the mess home and up to the kitchen.

Wave to husband — in hat and scarf, up in Barbecue Heaven, frantically fanning coals with a hair dryer — then dive immediately into Bourbon Squash Rings and Cranberry Orange Muffins.

Stuff turkey, despite lack of cavity in which to stuff stuffing, or thread strong enough to sew it up. Decide nylon kite string might melt, then cut cotton cords off child's pull-duck toy and wind round turkey mummy-fashion, until it looks like macramé boat bumper.

Since hardware store won't have heard of cheesecloth and sold you dishrag instead, dip same in butter and pat round turkey aka Really Stunning Entrée, and haul up ladder to barbecue and sling on, noting that it covers entire grill area like a living mass of bread dough and that black domed lid of Webber perches on it like a too-small bowler hat. Secure by smashing lid down flush with the bird and twisting wire coat hangers around it.

Undo every 10 minutes when (according to barbecue book you might want to pitch with happy cookout group on cover smiling down at a perfect golden turkey) you're supposed to add another briquette. If you have any. Or when you want to take just one more peek because you've never seen so much smoke in your life, all of which is snaking through the open Velux windows into the living room, making the festively-laid table invisible.

Dig into attic for fans. Rig microphone stand and golf umbrella over Webber to keep you dry (until wind sends umbrella down into next door's yew hedge).

Greet guests: mostly Brits never having celebrated Thanksgiving before, nervous they'll be asked to pray a lot (not a bad idea), and intrigued by idea of whole turkey sizzling up on barbecue. Smile reassuringly while tending hanger burns under cold tap, taking meat thermometer readings by flashlight, and catching pneumonia. Announce you'll be eating by about Christmas and push hors d'oeuvres in a big way.

Do not panic when husband yells. Do not use fire extinguisher. Suppress shrieks when antique platter bites the dust (lose high heels on ladder) and turkey slides down roof slates. Retrieve from crevice on lower roof terrace, remove leaves and debris, and decide turkey resembles relic from Pompeii, having spent a year in Vesuvius. Herald entrance into dining room with kazoo. Find hacksaw and carve.

Make short speech about Pilgrim Fathers' first Thanksgiving in 1621, in case anyone's wondering what exactly they're supposed to be giving thanks for today, outside of not breaking some bridgework or the house burning down, and serve. Don't forget cranberry sauce. And whatever's in the oven.

One Year Later

Read in a magazine there's a way of cooking fish in your dishwasher or a pot roast on the engine of your car and wonder if this could work with turkey (say, on someone else's car).

Contributed by ASTRID KING/ASTRID RONNING

feathered and furred game recipes

Lapin de tocqueville

When our friend Alison booked a wing of the Chateau de Tocqueville in Normandy for her family holiday a decade or so ago, she hadn't realised quite how much room she would have available. When she offered us the use of one of the spare bedrooms, we accepted with grateful visions of seafood lunches in exquisite harbour-side bistros in Barfleur and gut-busting dinners in the auberges between there and Cherbourg. Eating out every day, because we could guarantee prices far lower and quality far higher than we could ever get in Blighty, was not only on the menu, it was the menu.

But when we arrived and saw the small but delightful kitchen with its glittering array of esoteric equipment, I began to change my mind. And when we visited the local market the next day, the change was complete.

Now I must confess that before arriving in Normandy, I knew nothing whatsoever about Alexis de Tocqueville (1805–59). For an equally benighted reader, he was one of the great historians, author of *De la Democratie en Amerique* and *L'Ancien Regime et la Revolution*, the latter having been written in the very château where I, in my ignorance, now stood and thought of strange things to do with globe artichokes.

Tocqueville's great-great-grandniece, and last of the noble family line, Marie-Henriette Tocqueville (who died in 1994), met us and showed us the wing which she let out to holiday-makers, the pond with its lonely swan, the huge old pigeonry (home now to a pair of kestrels and their young, whose first flights we witnessed) and the equally huge, unfriendly German shepherd dog who made every short walk from car to château door such a tense and thrilling experience.

But to the market. Smaller items of meat still on the hoof or claw, vegetables that started in size and quality where most British produce leaves off but at prices that wouldn't buy you a globe artichoke here, even with its leaves off.

Then there was the rabbit. The only one I saw that wasn't still wearing its coat and running round in it. It lay rather forlornly on the stall at the end of the day, a couple of equally naked chickens keeping it company from a respectful distance. I like rabbit and I was beginning to think of some rustic stew like mother used to make. The farmer's wife came straight from cliché-land, rotund and rosy-cheeked, and she obviously thought I came from the same place, under the heading of stupid English townie tourist. Indeed, my French is pretty merde, as she could obviously tell from the way I said "Combien?"

- "C'est un lapin, m'sieur," she warned me, obviously under the impression I wanted a chicken.

- "Er….oui…combien le lapin?"

She looked at me suspiciously, concluded that I hadn't understood the word and had simply repeated it under the impression it meant chicken. She had an idea. She repeated the word again but this time with her hands sticking up at the sides of her head as ears and hopping back and forth behind her stall.

"Oui, oui. Lapin". Rabbit. "D'accord", I said, doing likewise myself and causing much amusement to the farmer's wife, my companions and quite a few villagers.

One of whom, ran another stall which had on it one large earthenware pot, full of .....what?

"Crème fraiche, m'sieur".

Wonderful, I thought, in another burst of ignorance. That will be nice with some fruit. Well, maybe for some, but I soon discovered that Normandy crème fraiche is a lot sourer than its Hampstead namesake. And I also discovered that Poire de Normandie, the local Perry, is a lot less drinkable than week-old bathwater.

And from such mistakes, great discoveries are made. So........

Lapin de tocqueville

Part of the inspiration for this dish was that we couldn't drink the Perry but we could cook with it. That led to the idea of using pears. And the fact that crème fraiche is now common in Blighty and, even more surprisingly, Poire de Normandie, can now be bought from Hampstead's very own La Reserve on Heath Street, means that we can present this recipe to the good burghers of NW3 without fear of frustration.

Serves 4

1 rabbit, preferably wild, jointed
seasoned plain flour, for dusting
vegetable oil or lard, for frying
white wine vinegar, for deglazing

1. Preheat the oven to 180°C/350°F/Gas Mark 4. Dust the rabbit joints with seasoned flour. In a flameproof, ovenproof casserole dish, fry the rabbit joints in the vegetable oil or melted lard until lightly browned all over, turning occasionally.

2. Remove from the casserole and set aside. Deglaze the casserole with a little wine vinegar.

250g (9oz) onions, thinly sliced
2 large pears, not too ripe, (such as William or Comice), peeled, cored and each cut into 6 or 8
wholegrain mustard (such as Meaux)
bouquet garni of fresh thyme, parsley and sage
1 bottle Poire de Normandie
2 tablespoons crème fraiche, preferably Norman (or soured cream, if preferred)

3. Place a layer of onions on the bottom of the casserole, then lay half the rabbit pieces on top. Place a layer of pear slices over the rabbit. Dollop on (as we say up north) a couple of teaspoons of grainy mustard and then repeat the three layers to use up all the ingredients. Place the bouquet garni on top.

4. Pour the booze into the pot, cover the casserole and stick it in the oven for 1 hour or so, until the rabbit is cooked and tender.

5. Remove from the oven, take out and discard the bouquet garni, pour off the juices and thicken them with the crème fraiche. Pour the sauce back into the casserole, reheat gently and serve hot. It goes well with mashed or baked potatoes and broccoli. And very well (I recently found) with a few glasses of well-chilled Fetzer's Californian Viognier.

Cook's Tips

If you want to be dead posh, the recipe can be adapted. Take the thigh bone out of a leg of rabbit (one per diner). Fry finely chopped shallots and make into a stuffing with chopped pear, sage and thyme, salt and pepper. Stuff the rabbit leg and wrap in Bayonne ham or pancetta. Tie with string. Cook in oil in a hot skillet for 10 minutes, turning occasionally, until cooked. Serve on potato gallettes with a sauce made from shallots, stock and Normandy Perry, flavoured with herbs and mustard, thickened with crème fraiche — and upgrade the wine to Condrieu.

Contributed by DAI LOWE

Quails *with port & cranberries*

Serves 4

4 oven-ready quails (1 quail per person)
4 rashers of unsmoked back bacon
(1 rasher per quail)
3 tablespoons sunflower oil
1 wineglass (about 250ml/9fl oz) of ruby port
3 mandorlas, blood oranges or other similar
orange/citrus fruit
100g (3½oz) fresh cranberries
salt and freshly ground black pepper

1. First order the quails and bacon from J.A. Steele.

2. Preheat the oven to 180°C/350°F/Gas Mark 4. Remove any trussing string from the quails. Heat the oil in a flameproof, ovenproof casserole dish, add the quails and cook until the breasts are brown, turning occasionally.

3. Stretch the bacon rashers thinly with a palette knife and tightly wrap each quail in bacon. Set aside.

4. Swill the pan with the port and bring it to the boil. Place the quails in a circle in the casserole. Divide the citrus fruit into quarters retaining the skin. Put a couple of segments between each quail. Throw in the cranberries and season with salt and pepper.

5. Cover with a lid and cook in the oven for 25–30 minutes, or until the quails are cooked and tender. Serve with richly creamed potatoes or garlic mash.

Contributed by DJS

Rabbit *with prunes & brandy*

Serves 6

2 rabbits, jointed
1 gammon steak (optional), cut into small cubes
300ml (½ pint) milk
1 blade of mace
1 bay leaf
few juniper berries
few fresh parsley stalks
3 tablespoons sunflower oil
100g (3½oz) red onion, chopped
2 sticks celery, chopped
250g (9oz) chestnut mushrooms, sliced
1 wine glass (250ml/9fl oz) of sweet sherry
1 wine glass (250ml/9fl oz) chicken stock or water
250g (9oz) prunes
50g (1¾oz) lexia raisins
salt and freshly ground black pepper
chopped fresh parsley, to garnish

1. Heat the milk in a saucepan with the blade of mace, bay leaf, juniper berries and parsley stalks, until almost boiling. Remove the pan from the heat and set aside until cool.

2. Lay the rabbit joints in a shallow dish and pour over the cooled milk. Cover and leave to marinade in a cool place for at least 2 hours. Drain the rabbit joints and discard the marinade. Pat the rabbit dry using kitchen paper.

3. Preheat the oven to 180°C/350°F/Gas Mark 4. Heat 2 tablespoons oil in a pan, add the onion and celery and sauté until lightly browned. Add the mushrooms and sauté until lightly browned. Remove the vegetables from the pan using a slotted spoon and place in an ovenproof casserole dish. Set aside.

4. Heat the remaining oil in the pan, add the rabbit joints and cook until lightly browned all over. If you are using gammon, brown it lightly in the pan, then add to the casserole.

5. Arrange the rabbit joints in a single layer over the vegetables (and gammon). Swill the cooking pan with the sherry, then add the stock or water. Add the prunes and raisins and bring the mixture to the boil. Season, then pour over the rabbit.

6. Cover and cook in the oven for about 1 hour, or until the rabbit is cooked and tender. Remove from the oven and allow to rest for 10 minutes, before serving. Garnish with chopped parsley. Serve with dauphinoise potatoes and green vegetables.

Contributed by DJS

Stuffed pheasant *with cream cheese & mushrooms*

Serves 4

225g (8oz) cream cheese
2–3 sticks celery, finely chopped
salt and freshly ground black pepper
2 oven-ready hen pheasants
225g (8oz) mushrooms, roughly chopped
2 cloves garlic, finely chopped
350g (12oz) shallots, halved
150ml (¼ pint) red wine

1. Preheat the oven to 200°C/400°F/Gas Mark 6. Mix together the cream cheese, celery and seasoning. Stuff the pheasants with the cream cheese mixture.

2. Mix the mushrooms and garlic together, then place them over the base of a roasting tin, covering the base completely.

3. Put the pheasants, breast-side down, on top of the mushrooms. Surround the pheasants with the shallot halves and pour the wine over the top.

4. Cover and bake in the oven for 30 minutes, then uncover and bake for a further 30–45 minutes, or until the pheasants are cooked, tender and nicely browned, turning them over once during cooking.

5. Serve with a dish of smooth mashed potatoes and a bowl of fresh watercress salad.

Contributed by DORIS LESSING

Pheasant *with morels and bacon*

Serves 2

1 pheasant
1 duck liver
1onion, chopped
50ml (2fl oz/½ cup) sunflower oil
salt and ground black pepper
4 slices bacon

For the Morel sauce
2 shallots, chopped
1 stalk of celery, chopped
50ml (2fl oz/½ cup) raspberry vinegar
100ml (4fl oz/1 cup) pheasant stock
100ml (4fl oz/1 cup) red wine
1 tablespoon chopped parsley
2 bay leaves
4 fresh morel mushrooms
knob of butter

1. Preheat oven to 220°C/425°F/Gas mark 7. Debone the pheasant (or get your butcher to do it for you!) and keep the flesh from its legs to make a stuffing with the duck liver.

Stuffing

2. Sauté the duck liver and the meat from the pheasant legs in a third of the oil with the chopped onion. Cool, season to taste and blend to make a paté-like mixture. Stuff this into the breast of the pheasant and hold closed with wooden cocktail sticks.

4. Cover the pheasant with the bacon and seal for 3 minutes in half the remaining oil in a hot frying pan. Cook in the oven for 20–25 minutes.

5. For the morel sauce, sauté the shallots and celery in the remaining oil, and add most of the raspberry vinegar. Add the stock, red wine, chopped parsley, bay leaves and mushrooms. Simmer to reduce for 5 minutes. Put the mushrooms to one side and pass the remaining ingredients through a sieve into a clean pan.

6. Reduce the sauce again for a minute or two. Add the mushrooms and butter and the remaining drop of raspberry vinegar. Heat through, and taste for seasoning.

7. Remove the pheasant from the oven and place on a board to rest for a few minutes. Slice it, place on a serving platter and pour the sauce over the meat. Serve with potato rissoles, caramelised baby turnips (navets) and braised chicory.

Contributed by LA CAGE IMAGINAIRE

Guide to roasting times

	Oven temperature	Time
Chicken	190°C/375°F/Gas 5	20 mins per 500g/lb + 20 mins
Poussin	90°C/375°F/Gas 5	40 to 45 mins total
Veal		
Well done	180°C/350°F/Gas 4	20 mins per 500g/lb
Pork		
Well done	180°C/350°F/Gas 4	25 mins per 500g/lb
Lamb		
Medium	180°C/350°F/Gas 4	20 mins per 500g/lb
Well done	180°C/350°F/Gas 4	25 mins per 500g/lb
Beef		
Rare	180°C/350°F/Gas 4	15 mins per 500g/lb
Medium	180°C/350°F/Gas 4	20 mins per 500g/lb
Well done	180°C/350°F/Gas 4	25 mins per 500g/lb
Duck	200°C/400°F/Gas 6	25 mins per 500g/lb
Goose	180°C/350°F/Gas 4	20 mins per 500g/lb + 20 mins
Pheasant	200°C/400°F/Gas 6	50 mins total
Venison	170°C/325°F/Gas 3	25 mins per 500g/lb
Turkey		
3.5–4.5kg/7–9lb	190°C/375°F/Gas 5	2½ hours total
5–6kg/10–12lb	190°C/375°F/Gas 5	3½–4 hours total
6.5–8.5kg/13–17lb	190°C/375°F/Gas 5	4½–5 hours total